I0500570

# Court House Records Research

## A Family Research Workbook

### Written By Catherine Coulter

Court House Records Research: A Family Research Workbook
Copyright © 2013 Catherine Coulter
All Rights Reserved
ISBN-13: 978-1482766929
ISBN-10: 1482766922

## Other Books Written By Catherine Coulter

My Family Tree Research Records

Family Group Research Records

Census Research Records

Cemetery and Funeral Home Research Records

Court House Research Records

Web Log and Web Accounts

## Books Written by Catherine Coulter under the name of Cathy Coulter

The Man in Red

A Children's Book of Poems Goodnight and Hello

## Introduction

In this book you will find research worksheets to help you with your research and listing where you found the records. This is so you can go back to view the records again or to note as an informational source. Take this book with you when you go a county court house to search for these records and record your findings in it.

The county court house records can be a great source of information for genealogists. Some of the records that can be found at county court houses are birth, marriage, deeds, death, and naturalization records. The information in these records will contain names and dates for these events but they can also give you other family members and information as well.

The date at which each county court house started recording these events will vary from county to county. Also keep in mind that as with townships, counties were created from other larger counties or regions. Records did not always change hands when this would happen. So you may need to check the dates that these changes occurred or when they started keeping these records. You may just find out that the records you are looking for are in another county.

Another reason for not finding records where you think they should be can very well be due to the fact that they could have been destroyed in a fire or flood. Whatever the reason you still may be able to find the information you need through historical societies, churches, cemeteries, and funeral homes to name a few. All in all these records are usually a great source of dates and information on your ancestors that makes it well worth looking into.

If it would help you, you can add tap dividers to the different sections in this book and label them accordingly.

## Birth Research Log/Record

Birth records usually will tell you where, when, and to whom a child was born. The Birth Record Log in this book is to help you at the court house when searching the birth records. It will help keep track of those you have found and those you still want to look for. It also will help you keep track of which county and state you have looked for your ancestors in. You can use these pages one page per surname if you wish.

There is a place for the first and last name of the ancestor you are looking for. There is a place for you to put the court house's book number that you will find the certificate information in as well as the page/certificate number for the birth record. The parents and birth date also has a space for each ancestor. If you already know this information this will help confirm that you have the right record. If not then you will be able to fill it in as you find the records.

May times there will be an index that will tell you which record book and page/certificate number to find the record in. This log will aid you in collecting the information on each individual you are looking for as you search the index. Once the log is competed it will give you a list of sources to use for verifying the records you have found. If you run out of time at the court house and need to go back at a later date to look at the certificate in the books you will not have to go through the index again. You will have all the information you will need already.

Getting a photo copy of the record often comes in handy and saves time at the court house. If for some reason you can't get a photo copy of the record you may be allowed to take a photo of it. This way if any questions come up on the notes you took you will not have to go back to the court house to look at it again.

# Birth Record

County of _____ State of _____

Last Name of Family_____

| Last Name | First Name | Book # | Page or Certificate # | Mother | Father | Date |
|---|---|---|---|---|---|---|
| | | | | | | |
| | | | | | | |
| | | | | | | |
| | | | | | | |
| | | | | | | |
| | | | | | | |
| | | | | | | |
| | | | | | | |
| | | | | | | |
| | | | | | | |
| | | | | | | |
| | | | | | | |
| | | | | | | |
| | | | | | | |
| | | | | | | |
| | | | | | | |
| | | | | | | |
| | | | | | | |
| | | | | | | |
| | | | | | | |
| | | | | | | |
| | | | | | | |
| | | | | | | |
| | | | | | | |
| | | | | | | |
| | | | | | | |
| | | | | | | |
| | | | | | | |
| | | | | | | |
| | | | | | | |
| | | | | | | |
| | | | | | | |

# Birth Record

County of _____ State of_____

Last Name of Family_____

| Last Name | First Name | Book # | Page or Certificate # | Mother | Father | Date |
|---|---|---|---|---|---|---|
| | | | | | | |
| | | | | | | |
| | | | | | | |
| | | | | | | |
| | | | | | | |
| | | | | | | |
| | | | | | | |
| | | | | | | |
| | | | | | | |
| | | | | | | |
| | | | | | | |
| | | | | | | |
| | | | | | | |
| | | | | | | |
| | | | | | | |
| | | | | | | |
| | | | | | | |
| | | | | | | |
| | | | | | | |
| | | | | | | |
| | | | | | | |
| | | | | | | |
| | | | | | | |
| | | | | | | |
| | | | | | | |
| | | | | | | |
| | | | | | | |
| | | | | | | |
| | | | | | | |
| | | | | | | |
| | | | | | | |
| | | | | | | |

# Birth Record

County of _____ State of _____

Last Name of Family_____

| Last Name | First Name | Book # | Page or Certificate # | Mother | Father | Date |
|---|---|---|---|---|---|---|
| | | | | | | |
| | | | | | | |
| | | | | | | |
| | | | | | | |
| | | | | | | |
| | | | | | | |
| | | | | | | |
| | | | | | | |
| | | | | | | |
| | | | | | | |
| | | | | | | |
| | | | | | | |
| | | | | | | |
| | | | | | | |
| | | | | | | |
| | | | | | | |
| | | | | | | |
| | | | | | | |
| | | | | | | |
| | | | | | | |
| | | | | | | |
| | | | | | | |
| | | | | | | |
| | | | | | | |
| | | | | | | |
| | | | | | | |
| | | | | | | |
| | | | | | | |
| | | | | | | |
| | | | | | | |
| | | | | | | |
| | | | | | | |
| | | | | | | |
| | | | | | | |

# Notes

## Marriage Record

The basic information you will find here is the bride's name, the groom's name, their age, and occupation. There should also be the name of the person who performed the marriage and even some times where the marriage took place in that county, as well as the occupations of the bride and groom. If either the bride or groom were under age at the time of the marriage then a separate document would be attached to the marriage record singed by a parent or next of kin to give consent to the marriage.

The Marriage Record Log in this book will help you at the court house when searching the marriage records. It will help keep track of those you have found and those you still want to look for. It also will help you keep track of which county and state you have looked for your ancestors. You can use these pages one page per surname if you wish. It has a place for the name of the bride, groom, and the marriage date.

The court house's book number and certificate number space will help you find the certificate information in as well as the page/certificate number for the marriage record. If you already know this information this will help confirm that you have the right record. If not then you will be able to fill it in as you find the records.

May times there will be an index that will tell you which record book and page/certificate number to find the record in. This log will aid you in collecting the information on each individual you are looking for as you search the index. Once the log is competed it will also give you a list of sources to use for verifying the records you have found. If you run out of time at the court house and need to go back at a later date to look at the certificates in the books you will not have to go through the index again. You will have all the information you will need already.

Getting a photo copy of the record often comes in handy and saves time at the court house. If for some reason you can't get a photo copy of the record you may be allowed to take a photo of it. This way if any questions come up on the notes you took you will not have to go back to the court house to look at it again.

# Marriage Records

County of _____ State of _____

Last Name of Family_____

| Bride | Groom | Date | Book # | Certificate # |
|-------|-------|------|--------|---------------|
|  |  |  |  |  |
|  |  |  |  |  |
|  |  |  |  |  |
|  |  |  |  |  |
|  |  |  |  |  |
|  |  |  |  |  |
|  |  |  |  |  |
|  |  |  |  |  |
|  |  |  |  |  |
|  |  |  |  |  |
|  |  |  |  |  |
|  |  |  |  |  |
|  |  |  |  |  |
|  |  |  |  |  |
|  |  |  |  |  |
|  |  |  |  |  |
|  |  |  |  |  |
|  |  |  |  |  |
|  |  |  |  |  |
|  |  |  |  |  |
|  |  |  |  |  |
|  |  |  |  |  |
|  |  |  |  |  |
|  |  |  |  |  |
|  |  |  |  |  |
|  |  |  |  |  |
|  |  |  |  |  |
|  |  |  |  |  |
|  |  |  |  |  |
|  |  |  |  |  |
|  |  |  |  |  |
|  |  |  |  |  |
|  |  |  |  |  |
|  |  |  |  |  |
|  |  |  |  |  |
|  |  |  |  |  |
|  |  |  |  |  |
|  |  |  |  |  |
|  |  |  |  |  |
|  |  |  |  |  |

# Marriage Records

County of _____ State of_____

Last Name of Family_____

| Bride | Groom | Date | Book # | Certificate # |
|-------|-------|------|--------|---------------|
|       |       |      |        |               |
|       |       |      |        |               |
|       |       |      |        |               |
|       |       |      |        |               |
|       |       |      |        |               |
|       |       |      |        |               |
|       |       |      |        |               |
|       |       |      |        |               |
|       |       |      |        |               |
|       |       |      |        |               |
|       |       |      |        |               |
|       |       |      |        |               |
|       |       |      |        |               |
|       |       |      |        |               |
|       |       |      |        |               |
|       |       |      |        |               |
|       |       |      |        |               |
|       |       |      |        |               |
|       |       |      |        |               |
|       |       |      |        |               |
|       |       |      |        |               |
|       |       |      |        |               |
|       |       |      |        |               |
|       |       |      |        |               |
|       |       |      |        |               |
|       |       |      |        |               |
|       |       |      |        |               |
|       |       |      |        |               |
|       |       |      |        |               |
|       |       |      |        |               |
|       |       |      |        |               |
|       |       |      |        |               |
|       |       |      |        |               |
|       |       |      |        |               |

# Marriage Records

County of _____ State of_____

Last Name of Family_____

| Bride | Groom | Date | Book # | Certificate # |
|-------|-------|------|--------|---------------|
|       |       |      |        |               |
|       |       |      |        |               |
|       |       |      |        |               |
|       |       |      |        |               |
|       |       |      |        |               |
|       |       |      |        |               |
|       |       |      |        |               |
|       |       |      |        |               |
|       |       |      |        |               |
|       |       |      |        |               |
|       |       |      |        |               |
|       |       |      |        |               |
|       |       |      |        |               |
|       |       |      |        |               |
|       |       |      |        |               |
|       |       |      |        |               |
|       |       |      |        |               |
|       |       |      |        |               |
|       |       |      |        |               |
|       |       |      |        |               |
|       |       |      |        |               |
|       |       |      |        |               |
|       |       |      |        |               |
|       |       |      |        |               |
|       |       |      |        |               |
|       |       |      |        |               |
|       |       |      |        |               |
|       |       |      |        |               |
|       |       |      |        |               |
|       |       |      |        |               |
|       |       |      |        |               |
|       |       |      |        |               |
|       |       |      |        |               |
|       |       |      |        |               |

# Notes

## Death Records

Death records may reveal next of kin, when and where they were born. They may also give if they were married and what occupation they had. It's possible that if they were in the military that too may be on record. Of course cause of death should be there as well, which would aid in starting a family medical history. Sometimes a last will and testament is available. This will give more information on family names and relationships.

The Death research log in this book will help you at the court house when searching for the death records. It will help keep track of those you have found and those you still want to look for. It also will help you keep track of which county and state you have looked for your ancestors. You can use these pages one page per surname if you wish.

The court house's book number and certificate number space will help you find the certificate information in as well as the page/certificate number for the death record. If you already know this information this will help confirm that you have the right record. If not then you will be able to fill it in as you find the information.

There may be an index that will tell you which record book and page/certificate number to find the record in. Once the log is competed it will also give you a list of sources to use for verifying the records you have found. If you run out of time at the court house and need to go back at a later date to find look at the certificates in the books you will not have to go through the index again. You will have all the information you will need already.

Getting a photo copy of the record often comes in handy and saves time at the court house. If for some reason you can't get a photo copy of the record you may be allowed to take a photo of it. This way if any questions come up on the notes you took you will not have to go back to the court house to look at it again.

# Death Research Log

County of_____ State of_____

Family of_____

| Name | Date of Death | Certificate # | Book # | Page # | Place of Death | Notes |
|---|---|---|---|---|---|---|
| | | | | | | |
| | | | | | | |
| | | | | | | |
| | | | | | | |
| | | | | | | |
| | | | | | | |
| | | | | | | |
| | | | | | | |
| | | | | | | |
| | | | | | | |
| | | | | | | |
| | | | | | | |
| | | | | | | |
| | | | | | | |
| | | | | | | |
| | | | | | | |
| | | | | | | |
| | | | | | | |
| | | | | | | |
| | | | | | | |
| | | | | | | |
| | | | | | | |
| | | | | | | |
| | | | | | | |
| | | | | | | |
| | | | | | | |
| | | | | | | |
| | | | | | | |
| | | | | | | |
| | | | | | | |
| | | | | | | |
| | | | | | | |
| | | | | | | |
| | | | | | | |
| | | | | | | |
| | | | | | | |

# Death Research Log

County of_____ State of_____

Family of_____

| Name | Date of Death | Certificate # | Book # | Page # | Place of Death | Notes |
|------|---------------|---------------|--------|--------|----------------|-------|
| | | | | | | |
| | | | | | | |
| | | | | | | |
| | | | | | | |
| | | | | | | |
| | | | | | | |
| | | | | | | |
| | | | | | | |
| | | | | | | |
| | | | | | | |
| | | | | | | |
| | | | | | | |
| | | | | | | |
| | | | | | | |
| | | | | | | |
| | | | | | | |
| | | | | | | |
| | | | | | | |
| | | | | | | |
| | | | | | | |
| | | | | | | |
| | | | | | | |
| | | | | | | |
| | | | | | | |
| | | | | | | |
| | | | | | | |
| | | | | | | |
| | | | | | | |
| | | | | | | |
| | | | | | | |
| | | | | | | |
| | | | | | | |
| | | | | | | |
| | | | | | | |
| | | | | | | |
| | | | | | | |
| | | | | | | |

# Death Research Log

County of_____ State of_____

Family of_____

| Name | Date of Death | Certificate # | Book # | Page # | Place of Death | Notes |
|------|---------------|---------------|--------|--------|----------------|-------|
|  |  |  |  |  |  |  |
|  |  |  |  |  |  |  |
|  |  |  |  |  |  |  |
|  |  |  |  |  |  |  |
|  |  |  |  |  |  |  |
|  |  |  |  |  |  |  |
|  |  |  |  |  |  |  |
|  |  |  |  |  |  |  |
|  |  |  |  |  |  |  |
|  |  |  |  |  |  |  |
|  |  |  |  |  |  |  |
|  |  |  |  |  |  |  |
|  |  |  |  |  |  |  |
|  |  |  |  |  |  |  |
|  |  |  |  |  |  |  |
|  |  |  |  |  |  |  |
|  |  |  |  |  |  |  |
|  |  |  |  |  |  |  |
|  |  |  |  |  |  |  |
|  |  |  |  |  |  |  |
|  |  |  |  |  |  |  |
|  |  |  |  |  |  |  |
|  |  |  |  |  |  |  |
|  |  |  |  |  |  |  |
|  |  |  |  |  |  |  |
|  |  |  |  |  |  |  |
|  |  |  |  |  |  |  |
|  |  |  |  |  |  |  |
|  |  |  |  |  |  |  |
|  |  |  |  |  |  |  |
|  |  |  |  |  |  |  |
|  |  |  |  |  |  |  |
|  |  |  |  |  |  |  |
|  |  |  |  |  |  |  |
|  |  |  |  |  |  |  |
|  |  |  |  |  |  |  |

# Notes

# Naturalization

As far as the naturalization records go they can be a bit tricky to find them all. A person coming to America wanting to become naturalized had several steps to go through before it became finalized.

The naturalization process changed over time and depending on the year you are searching you will need to be aware of the rules. There were a minimum number of years an immigrant had to have been in America and a minimum number of years they had to have lived in the state where they wanted to start the process before they could. Then after the intent to become naturalized had been filed there was another wait until they could file naturalization papers. During this time period they could move to another state and file the final naturalization papers there. They also had to have references from someone who was already a citizen.

Now citizenship for children and the wives were in connection with that of the husband/father. The fact that a child born in America was not always considered being a citizen upon birth even if the parents were not. That came into law eventually. If a child was under a certain age when their father became a citizen then they too gained citizenship. If not then they had to go through the process as well if they were to be considered a citizen.

If you know the date of naturalization or approximant year you can search the internet for the requirements for citizenship for that time period. It helps knowing this information because it could very well tell you what year your ancestor immigrated and just how long he resided in a particular state.

The Naturalization Research Log in this book will help you at the court house when searching for the naturalization records. It will help keep track of those you have found and those you still want to look for. It also will help you keep track of which county and state you have looked for your ancestors. You can use these pages one page per surname if you wish. Once the log is competed it will also give you a list of sources to use for verifying the records you have found. I have included a section as well for the recording of naturalization information that could be found on a naturalization petition.

Getting a photo copy of the record often comes in handy and saves time at the court house. If for some reason you can't get a photo copy of the record you may be allowed to take a photo of it. This way if any questions come up on the notes you took you will not have to go back to the court house to look at it again.

# Naturalization Research Log

County of _____ State of_____

| Last Name | First Name | Birthdate | Date of Immigration | Location of Record |
|-----------|-----------|-----------|---------------------|--------------------|
|           |           |           |                     |                    |
|           |           |           |                     |                    |
|           |           |           |                     |                    |
|           |           |           |                     |                    |
|           |           |           |                     |                    |
|           |           |           |                     |                    |
|           |           |           |                     |                    |
|           |           |           |                     |                    |
|           |           |           |                     |                    |
|           |           |           |                     |                    |
|           |           |           |                     |                    |
|           |           |           |                     |                    |

# Naturalization Research Log

County of _____ State of_____

| Last Name | First Name | Birthdate | Date of Immigration | Location of Record |
|-----------|-----------|-----------|--------------------|--------------------|
|  |  |  |  |  |
|  |  |  |  |  |
|  |  |  |  |  |
|  |  |  |  |  |
|  |  |  |  |  |
|  |  |  |  |  |
|  |  |  |  |  |
|  |  |  |  |  |
|  |  |  |  |  |
|  |  |  |  |  |
|  |  |  |  |  |
|  |  |  |  |  |

# Naturalization Research Records

County of _____ State of_____

Location of Record Found_____

_____

If you already know this information this will help confirm that you have the right record. If not, then you will be able to fill it in as you find the records.

| Full Name | |
|---|---|
| Date of Birth | Place of Birth |
| Occupation | |

Current Residence at Time of Petition_____

| Wife's Name | | Birthdate | |
|---|---|---|---|
| Child's Name | | Birthdate | |
| Child's Name | | Birthdate | |
| Child's Name | | Birthdate | |
| Child's Name | | Birthdate | |
| Child's Name | | Birthdate | |
| Child's Name | | Birthdate | |

| Date of Petition | District Court | Immigrated To | Emigrated From | Date of Emigration |
|---|---|---|---|---|
| | | | | |

| Port of Arrival | Date of Arrival | Name of Vessel |
|---|---|---|
| | | |

Witnessess_____

_____

_____

## Notes:

# Naturalization Research Records

County of _____ State of_____

Location of Record Found_____

_____

If you already know this information this will help confirm that you have the right record. If not, then you will be able to fill it in as you find the records.

| Full Name | |
|---|---|
| Date of Birth | Place of Birth |
| Occupation | |

Current Residence at Time of Petition_____

| Wife's Name | | Birthdate | |
|---|---|---|---|
| Child's Name | | Birthdate | |
| Child's Name | | Birthdate | |
| Child's Name | | Birthdate | |
| Child's Name | | Birthdate | |
| Child's Name | | Birthdate | |
| Child's Name | | Birthdate | |

| Date of Petition | District Court | Immigrated To | Emigrated From | Date of Emigration |
|---|---|---|---|---|
| | | | | |

| Port of Arrival | Date of Arrival | Name of Vessel |
|---|---|---|
| | | |

Witnessess_____

_____

_____

## Notes:

# Naturalization Research Records

County of _____ State of_____

Location of Record Found_____

_____

If you already know this information this will help confirm that you have the right record. If not, then you will be able to fill it in as you find the records.

| Full Name | | | |
|---|---|---|---|
| Date of Birth | | Place of Birth | |
| Occupation | | | |

Current Residence at time of petition_____

| Wife's Name | | Birthdate | |
|---|---|---|---|
| Child's Name | | Birthdate | |
| Child's Name | | Birthdate | |
| Child's Name | | Birthdate | |
| Child's Name | | Birthdate | |
| Child's Name | | Birthdate | |
| Child's Name | | Birthdate | |

| Date of Petition | District Court | Immigrated To | Emigrated From | Date of Emigration |
|---|---|---|---|---|
| | | | | |

| Port of Arrival | Date of Arrival | Name of Vessel |
|---|---|---|
| | | |

Witnessess_____

_____

_____

**Notes:**

# Naturalization Research Records

County of _____ State of _____

Location of Record Found_____

_____

If you already know this information this will help confirm that you have the right record. If not, then you will be able to fill it in as you find the records.

| Full Name | |
|---|---|
| Date of Birth | | Place of Birth | |
| Occupation | |

Current Residence at time of petition_____

| Wife's Name | | Birthdate | |
|---|---|---|---|
| Child's Name | | Birthdate | |
| Child's Name | | Birthdate | |
| Child's Name | | Birthdate | |
| Child's Name | | Birthdate | |
| Child's Name | | Birthdate | |
| Child's Name | | Birthdate | |

| Date of Petition | District Court | Immigrated To | Emigrated From | Date of Emigration |
|---|---|---|---|---|
| | | | | |

| Port of Arrival | Date of Arrival | Name of Vessel |
|---|---|---|
| | | |

Witnessess_____

_____

_____

**Notes:**

# Naturalization Research Records

County of _____ State of_____

Location of Record Found_____

_____

If you already know this information this will help confirm that you have the right record. If not, then you will be able to fill it in as you find the records.

| | |
|---|---|
| Full Name | |
| Date of Birth | | Place of Birth | |
| Occupation | |

Current Residence at time of petition_____

| | | | |
|---|---|---|---|
| Wife's Name | | Birthdate | |
| Child's Name | | Birthdate | |
| Child's Name | | Birthdate | |
| Child's Name | | Birthdate | |
| Child's Name | | Birthdate | |
| Child's Name | | Birthdate | |
| Child's Name | | Birthdate | |

| Date of Petition | District Court | Immigrated To | Emigrated From | Date of Emigration |
|---|---|---|---|---|
| | | | | |

| Port of Arrival | Date of Arrival | Name of Vessel |
|---|---|---|
| | | |

Witnessess_____

_____

_____

## Notes:

## Land/Deeds

The land/deed research log in this book will help you at the court house when searching for the land records. It will help keep track of those you have found and those you still want to look for. It also will help you keep track of which county and state you have searched land/deed records for your ancestors. You can use these pages one page per surname if you wish.

The indexes for the land/deed records are most likely are listed under the grantor or grantee's names. The term grantor means the person who is selling the land. The grantee is the person buying the land. You will then have to search them page by page to find your ancestor. You can put the ancestor's name you want to look for in the right column before you go to the court house and then you will have every one you want to search for on hand. I advise putting the names in alphabetical order to make searching easier. You will be able to fill the rest of this information in as you find the records.

Once the log is competed it will also give you a list of sources to use for verifying the records you have found. If you run out of time at the court house and need to go back at a later date to look at the land/deed records you will have all the information you will need already to locate them.

Land /deed records can be useful in searching for information on your ancestors but don't be surprised if you don't always find land records for some. As with today, some of our ancestors did not always own the land they lived on. Some rented land and homes, some were borders and then there were the ancestors who were employees of the people who owned the land. Searching for land/deeds is still worth doing because of the potential information that you may gain.

One piece of information that you will be able find is the date they bought the land. Keep in mind that the date may not be the exact date they moved on to the land. It dose though give you an approximant date that they came to that county. If they were coming from far away the husband of a family would sometimes come by himself to check out the area and buy some land for his family and at a later date they would move there. Sometimes the delay in moving on to the land was because they needed to save up some more money to travel to the newly acquired land and build a home.

The land records usually give the place where they lived at the time they bought the land. This will help document their residency there and possibly give you clues as to where to look for them next. It is always a good idea to check the land records where they had been living at the time of the sale to see if they owned land before. It will give you an idea where they lived before that as well. It establishes a trail for you to follow. Keep in mind that just because they left one place to move somewhere else does not mean they didn't move back to the same area that they left so it makes sense to look completely through the land/deed records and not stop when you find one record.

Another thing to keep in mind is that just because they moved on to a different place does not mean they sold the land they left before they left it or gave it to someone else. It is possible that they sold it later after the move. It then stands to reason that it is a good idea to search for the sale of this land as well as when they bought it.

You can learn how much land they owned and where it's located or a brief description of it. Farmers sometimes would also buy more land around or nearby later on in order to expand the farm. Sometimes their grown children would buy land adjacent to or nearby their parents to raise their own family and farm for themselves. The grown children may even add their land to their parents and thus continue to farm with their parents while expanding the family farm.

The land records will also tell you who sold them the land. Don't be surprised to find a parent or relative either sold or gifted them with land. This could be useful for you as well. It will include the price they paid for the land, if it was not a gift, and how many acres were sold.

One of your ancestors, if they had been in the military during the Revolutionary War or the War of 1812 very well could have received land for their service as a form of payment. In this situation you may find more information about him. You may find not only his residence but information on his enlistment. The information could be as simple as which company or regiment he was in to how long he was enlisted and his rank. If he actually moved on to that land it could be the reason he moved. He may have sold the land or gifted it to someone, just because he received a bounty land does not necessarily mean he kept it or lived on it.

# Land/Deed Log

County of _____ State of_____

Last Name of Family_____

| Grantor | Grantee | Book# | Page # | Date |
|---------|---------|-------|--------|------|
|  |  |  |  |  |
|  |  |  |  |  |
|  |  |  |  |  |
|  |  |  |  |  |
|  |  |  |  |  |
|  |  |  |  |  |
|  |  |  |  |  |
|  |  |  |  |  |
|  |  |  |  |  |
|  |  |  |  |  |
|  |  |  |  |  |
|  |  |  |  |  |
|  |  |  |  |  |
|  |  |  |  |  |
|  |  |  |  |  |
|  |  |  |  |  |
|  |  |  |  |  |
|  |  |  |  |  |
|  |  |  |  |  |
|  |  |  |  |  |
|  |  |  |  |  |
|  |  |  |  |  |
|  |  |  |  |  |
|  |  |  |  |  |
|  |  |  |  |  |
|  |  |  |  |  |
|  |  |  |  |  |
|  |  |  |  |  |
|  |  |  |  |  |
|  |  |  |  |  |
|  |  |  |  |  |
|  |  |  |  |  |
|  |  |  |  |  |
|  |  |  |  |  |
|  |  |  |  |  |
|  |  |  |  |  |
|  |  |  |  |  |

# Land/Deed Log

County of _____ State of_____

Last Name of Family_____

| Grantor | Grantee | Book# | Page # | Date |
|---------|---------|-------|--------|------|
| | | | | |
| | | | | |
| | | | | |
| | | | | |
| | | | | |
| | | | | |
| | | | | |
| | | | | |
| | | | | |
| | | | | |
| | | | | |
| | | | | |
| | | | | |
| | | | | |
| | | | | |
| | | | | |
| | | | | |
| | | | | |
| | | | | |
| | | | | |
| | | | | |
| | | | | |
| | | | | |
| | | | | |
| | | | | |
| | | | | |
| | | | | |
| | | | | |
| | | | | |
| | | | | |
| | | | | |
| | | | | |
| | | | | |
| | | | | |
| | | | | |
| | | | | |
| | | | | |

# Land/Deed Log

County of _____ State of_____

Last Name of Family_____

| Grantor | Grantee | Book# | Page # | Date |
|---------|---------|-------|--------|------|
|  |  |  |  |  |
|  |  |  |  |  |
|  |  |  |  |  |
|  |  |  |  |  |
|  |  |  |  |  |
|  |  |  |  |  |
|  |  |  |  |  |
|  |  |  |  |  |
|  |  |  |  |  |
|  |  |  |  |  |
|  |  |  |  |  |
|  |  |  |  |  |
|  |  |  |  |  |
|  |  |  |  |  |
|  |  |  |  |  |
|  |  |  |  |  |
|  |  |  |  |  |
|  |  |  |  |  |
|  |  |  |  |  |
|  |  |  |  |  |
|  |  |  |  |  |
|  |  |  |  |  |
|  |  |  |  |  |
|  |  |  |  |  |
|  |  |  |  |  |
|  |  |  |  |  |
|  |  |  |  |  |
|  |  |  |  |  |
|  |  |  |  |  |
|  |  |  |  |  |
|  |  |  |  |  |
|  |  |  |  |  |
|  |  |  |  |  |
|  |  |  |  |  |
|  |  |  |  |  |
|  |  |  |  |  |

# Notes

# Notes

www.ingramcontent.com/pod-product-compliance
Lightning Source LLC
Chambersburg PA
CBHW080736290526
45790CB00008B/3221